Hello

It is hard to believe that 30 years have passed since Kathy and I set off on our journey with Bubbie. Despite all the difficulties we faced and the challenges we met and overcame in the three decades since, neither of us ever regretted the adventure.

Kathy and I spent many happy hours in the kitchen. In addition to preparing the daily family meals, we loved tasting pickles for quality and consistency, and we tried a slew of new products and recipes.

We discovered that our time in the kitchen was refreshing and therapeutic, a chance to connect with each other while shifting our focus away from the stresses of business, and the intrusion of accounting and emails.

With the concept of "kitchen therapy" in mind, on the occasion of Bubbies 30th anniversary, our whole Bubbies family is excited and delighted to share the 35 recipes in this first Bubbies cookbook with you, a gift of taste and love from our family to yours.

As we developed our original 30 Bubbies recipes (one for each year) I wanted to celebrate Kathy by adding four of her favorite and most requested recipes as well as one of mine – the sweet hot mustard – a recipe I got in college.

And when I say "requests," I mean, "demands." Kathy would get imploring phone calls from relatives all over the country for her Chocolate Walnut Tart... "so rich it can make you sweat!" And the great flavor, color, and crunch of her tuna salad makes it the standard to beat.

(Those of you who have been counting will note that it's a total of 35 recipes in recognition of our 30th anniversary. So shoot me!)

Please enjoy this book and share it with your loved ones – with our best wishes for your health and happiness, plus liberal doses of kitchen therapy.

John M. Gray

Founder & CEO
Katalina Holding Company
Fall, 2018

Credits

Stephen Rustad
Creative Direction & Production
Rustadmarketing.com
steve@rustadmarketing.com

Emily Somple
Producer, Recipe Developer, Editor
Emilysomple.com
emmysomple@gmail.com

Alan Campbell
Director of Photography
& Art Direction
Alancampbellphotography.com
acpfoto@gmail.com

Joanna Bodano
Food & Prop Stylist, Recipe Developer
Stylingbyjoanna.com
stylingbyjoanna@pacbell.net
Valerie Valdivia

Artwork
Valerievaldivia.com
info@valerievaldivia.com

Colleen Rustad
Copywriting
Rustadmarketing.com
colleen@rustadmarketing.com

Randall Chet
Graphic Design & Layout
Southpaw-design.com
randallchet@gmail.com

Brian Cary
Camera & Production Assistant
Photobac.com
brian@brianacary.com

Printed in China

First Printing, 2018
ISBN: 978-0-578-49917-8
Library of Congress Control Number: 201994014

Bubbies Fine Foods LLC
4125 Market St., Suite 1
Ventura, CA 93003

www.Bubbies.com

Recipes

BREAKFAST

Maple Sweet Potato
and Chorizo Hash
Page 9

Smoked Salmon
Spread
Page 10

Beet Hollandaise
Eggs Benedict
Page 12

Bacon
Frittata
Page 15

APPETIZERS

Cornmeal Crusted
Calamari
Page 19

Bubbies
Tuna Salad
Page 20

Mini
Lobster Rolls
Page 23

Festive
Crab Dip
Page 24

Fresh Corn
Fritters
Page 27

Reuben
Biscuits
Page 28

Creamy Dill
Potato Soup
Page 30

Tomato Soup and
Grilled Cheese Toasts
Page 33

COCKTAILS

Pickled
Bloody Mary
Page 37

Dill
Gin and Tonic
Page 38

Pickled
Whiskey Sour
Page 41

Dirty
Spicy Martini
Page 42

ENTREES & SIDES

DESSERTS

KATHY'S FAVORITES

"Skipping breakfast?
Not in my house!"

Breakfast

Maple Sweet Potato and Chorizo Hash

If hash brings to mind a diner dish made with leftovers from
the back of the refrigerator fried up with potatoes into a meal
so heavy it would sink the Titanic, have I got a treat for you! My hash is fresh,
colorful, and full of delicious textures and flavors...and so pretty too, with a sunny egg
on top! Orange sweet potatoes, spicy sausage, a hint of maple, and tangy sauerkraut
all blend beautifully in a one-pan wonder perfect for breakfast or dinner.

Ingredients:

2 small sweet potatoes — *cleaned and cubed*

2 small russet potatoes — *cleaned and cubed*

1 onion — *sliced*

3 tablespoons maple syrup

2 tablespoons olive oil

2-3 links smoked chorizo sausage
— *sliced (about 1 ½-2 cups)*

1 ½ cups **Bubbies Naturally
Fermented Spicy Sauerkraut**

4 eggs

Salt & Pepper to taste

Directions:

1. Preheat oven to 400 degrees.

2. Cube potatoes and toss with olive oil, maple syrup, and salt. Place on a parchment-lined baking sheet in oven for 15-20 minutes until golden brown.

3. In a large cast-iron or oven-safe skillet, sauté onion in olive oil for 5-8 minutes until caramelized. Add sausage and sauté 5-8 more minutes.

4. When potatoes are done, add to pan with onions, and sausage. Mix in 1 cup sauerkraut. Crack 4 eggs into pan, then place in middle of oven with broiler on for 5 minutes until eggs are cooked. Top with the remaining fresh spicy sauerkraut and serve.

Serves 4 people • Total Preparation Time 25 minutes

Smoked Salmon Spread

Whoever had the bright idea to spread cool cream cheese on a chewy bagel and top it with salty smoked salmon deserves a special place in culinary history. It's a perfect combination, but I'm always thinking about how to add more flavor, improve the presentation, or make a dish more versatile. I hope you'll agree that this recipe accomplishes all those things. A spoonful of my Horseradish cuts through the richness of the cream cheese. Blending it into a spread means you can keep it on hand for a quick breakfast or an impromptu cocktail party. Perhaps you can improve upon perfection?

Ingredients:

8 ounces cream cheese — *softened*

½ cup créme fraîche

2 tablespoons **Bubbies Prepared Horseradish**

2 tablespoons dill — *chopped*

2 tablespoons fresh chives

2 tablespoons fresh lemon juice

8 ounces smoked salmon

Directions:

1. Put all ingredients into food processor, and pulse 4-6 times until well incorporated.

2. Taste and adjust seasoning if necessary. Transfer to a small bowl and serve with toasted bagels or sliced artisan bread.

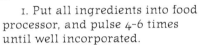

Serves 4 people • Total Preparation Time 10 minutes

Beet Hollandaise Eggs Benedict

We all know that Eggs Benedict isn't something you're going to whip up on a weekday morning before taking the kids to school. The dish requires strategic timing in the preparation of the components so that the poached eggs and creamy hollandaise – along with the toast, asparagus, and avocado – are stacked and served warm, dripping with velvety richness. While this is a challenging recipe, the rewards outweigh the risks when you serve this scrumptiously beautiful dish for a weekend brunch. Get ready for oohs and aahs and Instagram fame.

Ingredients:

4 slices Artisan bread – *brushed with olive oil and toasted*

1 bunch asparagus (12-15 stalks) – *trimmed*

4 slices prosciutto

4 eggs – *poached*

2 egg yolks

1 stick (½ cup) unsalted butter

1 tablespoon fresh lemon juice

2 tablespoons **Bubbies Beet Horseradish**

1 avocado – *mashed with a squeeze of lemon juice*

1 tablespoon of vinegar

1 tablespoon fresh chives – *chopped*

Salt and freshly ground pepper

Directions:

1. Heat oven to 400 degrees. Lightly toast bread.

2. Divide asparagus into 4 portions and wrap each with slice of prosciutto around middle of bundle. Place each bundle on a baking sheet pan lined with parchment paper.

3. Brush each bundle of asparagus with olive oil. Sprinkle with salt and freshly ground pepper. Cook for about 10 minutes until prosciutto is crispy and asparagus is cooked.

4. Fill a large saucepan half full of water. Add 1 tablespoon vinegar and bring to simmer for poached eggs.

5. While asparagus is cooking, make hollandaise: In a small pan melt 1 stick butter; set aside. In a medium saucepan heat 2 inches of water until simmering, then reduce heat to low.

6. Place egg yolks in a medium glass bowl. Place bowl over water in medium saucepan. Whisk egg yolks until mixture bubbles at edges, then add lemon juice.

7. Slowly whisk in melted butter until all butter is incorporated. Keep whisking into a nice, smooth, thick sauce. Next, slowly whisk in the beet horseradish. Taste and adjust seasoning with salt and freshly ground pepper; add more lemon juice if necessary.

Serves 4 people • Total Preparation Time 35 minutes

8. Immediately place sauce into a thermos with a lid to keep warm until ready to use. Or leave in bowl and cover with plastic wrap and keep warm. Just don't continue to cook it.

9. In a small bowl mash avocado with a bit of fresh lemon juice, salt, and freshly ground pepper.

10. Now make poached eggs: Crack 1 egg into a small bowl and gently add to simmering water. Continue with remaining eggs. Cook for 3-4 minutes, remove with a slotted spoon and gently set aside on warm plate.

11. To serve: top each toast with avocado mash, then a bundle of asparagus, followed by the egg, and finally a nice drizzle of beet horseradish hollandaise. Garnish with fresh chives, salt, and freshly ground pepper.

Bacon Frittata

Economical, packed with protein, quick to prepare, and versatile, eggs are practically the perfect food. All those star qualities are deliciously represented in this Bacon Frittata. Think of this recipe as a template; you won't go wrong using whatever cheese, vegetables or leftover meat you have in your fridge. Topped with Spicy Sauerkraut — which amazingly has zero calories — for its kick and healthful qualities, the frittata is an easy anytime meal.

Ingredients:

1 cup bacon lardons — 3-4 *pieces*

1 small shallot

½ cup **Bubbies Naturally Fermented Spicy Sauerkraut**

1 garlic clove — *minced*

1 tablespoon fresh chives

1 tablespoon fresh thyme

½ cup shredded Gruyère cheese

1 cup of mushrooms — *sliced*

8 eggs

2 tablespoons water or milk

Directions:

1. Preheat oven to 400 degrees.

2. Chop bacon and cook in a skillet on medium high heat for 5-7 minutes until done. Place on paper towel and set aside.

3. In same skillet, cook shallot, garlic, mushrooms and herbs over medium high heat for 5 minutes.

4. In a large mixing bowl, crack eggs and whisk well with water or milk. Add bacon, cheese, and mushroom mixture to the eggs and combine well.

5. Pour mixture into oven-safe pie pan or casserole dish. Bake for 15-20 minutes or until center has set.

6. Serve topped with fresh spicy sauerkraut.

Serves 4-5 people • Total Preparation Time 30 minutes

"A tasty appetizer is the promise of a good dinner."

Appetizers

Cornmeal Crusted Calamari

Mention calamari and you usually get a "love it or leave it" response. But these crispy, golden-brown rings served with Spicy Horseradish Aioli have made believers out of many former calamari doubters. The key is to cook the calamari rings only until they are just golden so that they stay tender and don't take on the texture of rubber bands. I suggest making the aioli sauce a day or two ahead and breading the calamari in advance. Then when your guests arrive, just heat the oil and fry 'em up. A pretty platter of calamari and aioli makes a beautiful centerpiece. Just add friends and a nice bottle of pinot gris, and you've got the perfect recipe for an evening of conviviality.

Ingredients:

½ cup mayonnaise

2-3 tablespoons **Bubbies Spicy Horseradish**

1 teaspoon fresh lemon juice

1 tablespoon fresh chives — *chopped*

1 ½ pounds calamari
— *cleaned, with bodies cut into ½ inch rings*

3 eggs

2 cups cornmeal

½ cup flour

2 teaspoons dried oregano

2 teaspoons garlic salt

1 cup oil
(avocado, coconut or other)
for frying

Salt and freshly ground black pepper

Directions:

1. To make aioli, combine mayonnaise, horseradish, lemon juice, chives, salt, and pepper in a small bowl. Cover and refrigerate until ready to use.

2. Mix cornmeal, flour, and spices in a shallow dish. Whisk eggs together in another shallow dish.

3. Dry calamari rings in a paper towel and lightly salt and pepper them. Have a baking sheet nearby to transfer calamari onto after dipping.

4. Take a small handful of calamari and dip into egg mixture, then into cornmeal mixture to coat. Shake off excess and transfer to baking sheet and continue with remaining rings.

5. Preheat oven to 180 degrees, and line a baking sheet with paper towels. This will keep the cooked calamari warm while frying.

6. To a large, deep skillet add desired oil about ¼- ½ inch deep. Heat over high heat to about 350 degrees. Add calamari, working in batches without crowding, and cook until golden brown on each side.

7. Remove with a slotted spoon to lined baking sheet, and keep warm in oven while frying remaining rings.

8. Serve warm with horseradish aioli.

Serves 4 people • Total Preparation Time 35 minutes

Bubbie's Tuna Salad

For those of us who grew up in homes that always had a couple of cans of tuna in the cupboard, this Tuna Salad recipe will be like meeting an old friend. If you haven't had the pleasure of mixing up a protein-packed tuna salad that has just the right balance of vinegary tang — thanks to my Dill Pickle Relish and a couple of tablespoons of lemon juice and capers — let me introduce you. This is the perfect dish to have on hand in the fridge for sandwiches, wraps or, if you're avoiding carbs, piled onto greens. Sometimes I serve it with sliced red potatoes for an international flair. Voilà! Salade Niçoise.

baby

Ingredients:

7 ounce jar of tuna packed in oil — *drained*

2 tablespoons **Bubbies Dill Pickle Relish** + 1 tablespoon brine

2 tablespoons capers — *chopped*

1 small garlic clove — *minced*

2 tablespoons kalamata olives — *chopped*

1 tablespoon shallot — *minced*

1 tablespoon olive oil

1 tablespoon freshly squeezed lemon juice

1 tablespoon fresh dill — *chopped*

1 tablespoon fresh chives — chopped

Freshly ground pepper

Directions:

1. In a medium bowl combine all ingredients. Adjust to desired taste with more pickle or lemon juice, or more fresh herbs if you like.

2. Serve in lettuce cups, with crackers, or as a salad topping. Or use for sandwiches or wraps.

Serves 2 people • Total Preparation Time 10 minutes

Mini Lobster Rolls

My hat is off to the first person brave enough to boil a lobster and then grab hold of the claw to get to the meat inside. Even today, eating a whole lobster can be an intimidating experience. First, you have to get over having your dinner stare back at you while, next, you're attempting to use the proper tool and technique to extract the delicate meat from the nooks and crannies. That's the beauty of lobster rolls. The sandwich delivery system makes lobster accessible to everyone at any kind of occasion. My recipe improves on the classic combination by adding Spicy Horseradish, pickle brine, and fresh herbs to the mayo dressing for added zest. The best part? No lobster bib required.

Ingredients:

One large or two small lobster tails — *about 12 ounces total*

4-6 mini brioche buns

⅓ cup mayonnaise

1 tablespoon **Bubbies Spicy Horseradish**

1 teaspoon **Bubbies Dill Pickle** brine

1 teaspoon fresh lemon juice

¼ cup celery from an inside tender stalk

1 teaspoon fresh dill — *chopped*

2 teaspoons fresh tarragon — *chopped*

1-2 drops hot sauce

Pinch of salt

Directions:

1. Place a medium pot fitted with a steamer and lid on stove with 2-3 inches of water. Bring to boil. Steam lobster tails for 5-7 minutes until meat is opaque and plump.

2. Remove and rinse under cold water. With kitchen shears, cut down the front of the shell to release the meat. Chop lobster meat into chunks, and set aside to cool.

3. In another bowl mix mayonnaise, horseradish, pickle brine, herbs, salt, and hot sauce. Gently mix in lobster. Taste and adjust seasoning if necessary.

4. Heat a large skillet over medium-high heat and toast the outside top and bottom of each bun, leaving the inside soft and ready to hold the lobster mixture.

5. Spoon a few tablespoons of lobster into each bun and serve.

Serves 4-6 people • Total Preparation Time 40 minutes

Festive Crab Dip

Like caviar, crab meat is a delicacy I splurge on for special occasions. For this sophisticated party dip, I blend the crab with a cheesy, rich sauce made with cream cheese, Gruyère, and half-and-half. Then I add Dijon mustard and my Spicy Horseradish for a little zing but not so much that it overpowers the sweet and tender crab. Just thinking about spreading this melty, creamy, savory combination on toasted sourdough makes my mouth water. So for your next celebration, spend a few extra dollars and serve my Crab Dip. Your guests will leave feeling like a million bucks.

Ingredients:

10-12 ounces fresh crab meat — *cleaned*

3 tablespoons **Bubbies Spicy Horseradish**

⅓ cup shallot — *minced*

1 garlic clove — *minced*

½ teaspoon Dijon mustard

½ teaspoon hot sauce

1 tablespoon fresh lemon juice

1 cup Gruyére cheese — *shredded*

8 ounces cream cheese
— *cut into small cubes*

½ cup half-and-half

½ teaspoon Old Bay seasoning

3 tablespoons butter

½ cup panko crumbs

¼ cup fresh chives — *chopped*

Pinch of salt and freshly ground pepper

Directions:

1. Gather all ingredients, then clean the crab. Preheat oven to 400 degrees.

2. In a medium saucepan melt 2 tablespoons butter and sautè the shallot and garlic for 2-3 minutes. Add Old Bay seasoning, then slowly add half-and-half and cream cheese cubes, whisking until incorporated.

3. Turn off heat and mix in Gruyére cheese until melted. Add horseradish, mustard, hot sauce, and freshly squeezed lemon juice.

4. Add crabmeat and 2 tablespoons chives. Taste and adjust to desired taste. Transfer mixture to an ovenproof baking dish and sprinkle with panko.

5. Place small pieces of the remaining tablespoon of butter around the top of the bread crumbs. Bake about 20 minutes until top is golden brown.

6. Garnish with remaining chives and serve warm with fresh bread, crostini, crackers or fresh vegetables.

Serves 6 people • Total Preparation Time 30 minutes

Fresh Corn Fritters

This recipe is so simple that you'll need to make it only once before you know it by heart. And you're going to be glad that Corn Fritters are in your recipe repertoire because these crispy little beauties — the colors remind me of confetti — can be enjoyed in so many ways. Serve these fritters with fried eggs for a satisfying breakfast or dinner. Whip up a batch as a quick side for grilled meats. Or top your fritters with salsa and sour cream for game-day snacks. Touchdown!

Ingredients:

2 cups fresh or frozen (thawed) corn

2 eggs

½ cup **Bubbies Dill Pickle Relish** — *drained of brine*

2 tablespoons créme fraiche

2 scallions — *finely chopped*

⅓ cup red pepper — *finely chopped*

½ cup cornmeal

¼ cup flour

3 Heirloom tomatoes

2 garlic cloves

1 tablespoon fresh basil

½ cup homemade aioli or mayonnaise

1 teaspoon freshly squeezed lemon juice

Olive oil

Salt and pepper

Directions:

1. To make dipping sauce: preheat oven to 400 degrees. Cut tomatoes in half and place on a parchment-lined baking sheet with garlic cloves; drizzle with olive oil and sprinkle with salt and pepper.

2. Roast for 20 minutes. Remove from oven and let cool. Remove skins from tomatoes and place in a bowl with garlic, basil, mayonnaise and lemon juice.

3. Use immersion blender to blend until smooth. Taste and adjust seasoning if necessary, then refrigerate.

4. To make corn fritters: combine corn, eggs, relish, créme fraiche, scallions, red pepper, cornmeal, and flour together. In a heavy skillet heat olive oil. Spoon batter into skillet, 2-3 tablespoons per corn cake. Cook until golden brown on each side, about 3-4 minutes per side.

Serves 6 people • Total Preparation Time 40 minutes

Reuben Biscuits

A Reuben sandwich is a masterpiece of culinary mash-ups. Salty Irish corned beef and crunchy German sauerkraut stacked on toasted Jewish rye oozing with melted Swiss cheese and tangy Russian dressing. So delicious but — oh my — so messy! I always end up with sauerkraut brine running down my arm. So for those occasions (think brunches and bridal showers) when you want to serve the unbeatable Reuben combination in a more manageable package, I created Reuben Biscuits. A mimosa in one hand and a Reuben Biscuit in the other — your guests won't ever want to leave.

Ingredients:

2 cups all-purpose flour

¾ teaspoon salt

1 tablespoon baking powder

2 teaspoons sugar

4 tablespoons unsalted butter — *chilled*

1 cup shredded Swiss cheese

¾ cup chopped corned beef or diced ham

⅓ cup well-drained **Bubbies Naturally Fermented Sauerkraut**

¼ cup sour cream

½ cup milk

2 tablespoons cream to brush on tops of biscuits

Directions:

1. Preheat oven to 425 degrees. Lightly grease a baking sheet or line it with parchment paper.

2. In a large bowl, whisk together flour, salt, baking powder, and sugar.

3. Cut butter into flour using a pastry cutter or fork until mixture resembles coarse crumbs.

4. Mix in cheese, meat, and sauerkraut until evenly distributed.

5. In a separate bowl, whisk together sour cream and milk and stir into dough. Note that dough will be sticky.

6. Drop dough by ¼-cupfuls onto prepared baking sheet, keeping biscuits about 1 inch apart. You can also press dough into a large round about 1 inch thick and use a 3-inch biscuit cutter to make evenly round biscuits.

7. Brush biscuits with cream. Bake for 22 to 24 minutes, until golden brown.

Makes 12 biscuits • Total Preparation Time 40 minutes

Creamy Dill Potato Soup

Nothing pleases me more than filling my kitchen with the aroma of soup simmering on the stove, especially when it reminds me of my beloved Kosher Dill Pickles. Creamy Dill, one of my favorite soup recipes, marries flavor, nourishment, satisfaction and the traditions of diverse cultures. The word "dill" comes from the Old Norse word *dylla,* meaning to soothe or lull. The ancient Romans considered dill to be good luck while the Egyptians used it as an aphrodisiac. And today? I think you'll agree with me that dill means delicious.

Ingredients:

2 tablespoons of butter

1 medium onion – *halved and sliced*

5 cups chicken or vegetable broth

5 large
Bubbies Kosher Dill Pickles,
– about 2 cups, chopped

⅔ cup pickle brine

4 large potatoes
– peeled and cut into ½ inch cubes

1 cup sour cream

Salt and pepper to taste

Fresh dill to garnish

Directions:

1. Melt butter in a large pot and sauté onion until translucent.

2. Stir in the broth, pickles, pickle brine, and potatoes. Bring to boil, reduce heat, and simmer until potatoes are tender, about 30 minutes.

3. Use an immersion blender, or transfer to a blender, and blend until smooth. Add sour cream and stir until creamy. Add salt and pepper to taste.

4. Garnish with a pickle slice and some fresh dill.

Serves 4-6 people • Total Preparation Time 45 minutes

Tomato Soup and Grilled Cheese Toasts

One time when I was young, I visited a friend and was invited to stay for lunch. Her mother said she was making tomato soup, ordinarily one of my favorite dishes. But in my friend's house, tomato soup came from a can. When we sat down to eat, it was only my good manners that kept me from saying, "You call this tomato soup? Where's the depth of flavor from the roasted tomatoes, the sweetness from the fennel balanced with the tang from the sauerkraut, and the toothsome texture?"

Yes, when it came to food, I was a precocious child. I hope you enjoy tomato soup like it should be made.

Ingredients:

10 Roma or heirloom tomatoes — *halved*

½ cup **Bubbies Naturally Fermented Sauerkraut** — *drained*

4 garlic cloves

2 large shallots — *chopped*

1 cup fennel — *chopped*

1 tablespoon fresh oregano

28-ounce can San Marzano tomatoes

1 cup water

1 teaspoon maple syrup or sugar

½ cup cream (optional)

4-6 slices of artisan bread

4 ounces of aged white cheddar — *sliced thin*

2 tablespoons olive oil

2 tablespoons fennel fronds — *chopped for garnish (optional)*

Salt and freshly ground pepper

Serves 4 people • Total Preparation Time 1 hour

Directions:

1. Heat oven to 250 degrees. Toss fresh tomatoes and garlic cloves with 1 tablespoon of olive oil, a pinch of salt, and pepper; place cut side down on parchment-lined baking sheet and roast for 1 hour. Remove from oven, cool briefly, and remove skins.

2. While tomatoes are roasting, in a soup pot heat 1 tablespoon olive oil over medium heat. Add shallot, fennel, salt, and pepper. Cook 3-5 minutes until soft.

3. Turn heat to low. Add oregano, and cook for a few more minutes. Add canned tomatoes and all the juice plus water and a bit of maple syrup or sugar. Continue to cook on low for 20 minutes.

4. Add roasted tomatoes and sauerkraut to pot and cook for 10 more minutes.

5. With immersion blender, puree soup to desired consistency. Taste and adjust seasoning if necessary. Add cream for a richer soup. Serve soup with a tablespoon of sauerkraut, some fennel fronds and a drizzle of olive oil. (If you prefer a smoother soup, strain it before adding cream).

6. To make grilled cheese toasts, preheat oven to Broil.

7. Place bread slices on parchment-lined baking sheet and brush with remaining olive oil. Place cheese slices on bread and broil until melted and slightly crispy.

8. Serve with freshly ground pepper alongside the tomato soup.

"L'Chiam (To life!)
Just don't overdo it, darling."

Cocktails

Pickled Bloody Mary

Bloody Marys are the perfect cocktail to serve for brunch because they jump-start everyone's appetite. The red in the glass stimulates hunger, the piquant tomato juice wakes up your taste buds, and the vodka, well, we all know what that does. While there are infinite variations on the amount of heat and seasoning in Bloody Mary recipes, adding my Spicy Horseradish and Spicy Dill Pickle brine creates, quite literally, an eye-opening twist on the classic cocktail that delivers the goods.

Ingredients:

28 ounces good quality tomato juice or Clamato juice

8 ounces vodka

2 tablespoons **Bubbies Spicy Horseradish**

2 tablespoons **Bubbies Spicy Dill Pickle** brine

3 tablespoons freshly squeezed lime juice

2 tablespoons freshly squeezed lemon juice

1-2 teaspoons Worcestershire sauce

1-2 teaspoons hot sauce

Salt and freshly ground pepper to taste

Tender celery stalks and pickle spears for garnish

Directions:

1. In a pitcher, whisk together all ingredients. Taste and adjust seasoning if necessary.

2. Pour into four 10-12 ounce glasses filled with ice, garnish and serve.

Makes 1 pitcher • Total Preparation Time 5 minutes

Dill Gin and Tonic

A tall gin and tonic over ice is everything you want in a summer cocktail...icy cold and pleasantly sharp. But sometimes even the classics can seem a little uninspired. To liven things up – after all, isn't that what a cocktail should do? – I kept the same simple recipe but added pickle brine. Our palate perceives both bitter and sour as refreshing so adding pickle brine makes the cocktail doubly invigorating. It's a mini-vacation in a glass.

Ingredients:

3 ounces (2 shots) gin (1 shot = 1.5 ounces)

1.5 ounces Bubbies Kosher Dill Pickle brine

1.5 ounces tonic

2 sprigs fresh dill

Bubbies Dill Pickle cut into a spear or other fun shape for garnish

Directions:

1. Place fresh dill in the shaker and muddle gently. Add all liquid ingredients and ice. Shake.

2. Strain into chilled cocktail glass and garnish with dill pickle spear and sprig of fresh dill.

Makes 1 cocktail • Total Preparation Time 5 min

Pickled Whiskey Sour

Cocktail historians agree that the first time a recipe for a whiskey sour appeared in print was in "The Bartender's Guide" written by Jerry Thomas and published in 1862. Made with just three ingredients — spirits, sweetener, and a citrus component — the basic whiskey sour combination is still delicious 150 years later. One day as I was getting out the shaker to make this classic cocktail, it struck me. It's a whiskey sour...it should be made with pickle brine! I think Jerry would approve.

Ingredients:

3 ounces (2 shots) whiskey (1 shot = 1.5 ounces)

1 ounce simple syrup

¾ ounce **Bubbies Bread and Butter Pickle** brine

Meyer lemon wedge for garnish

Directions:

1. Place all liquid ingredients in a cocktail shaker. Fill with ice and shake.

2. Press lemon wedge around inside of a cocktail glass.

3. Strain liquid into glass and garnish with lemon wedge.

Makes 1 cocktail • Total Preparation Time 5 minutes

Dirty Spicy Martini

Martinis have long been perceived as the cocktail for the urbane and sophisticated. But sometimes mixologists – or "bartenders" as they were known in my day – get a little pretentious with their martini recipes. You know, the whole "shaken, not stirred" thing. That's why I thought I would have a little fun with the iconic vodka martini. In this lip-smacking variation, I added brine from my Spicy Dill Pickles for a salty and slightly cloudy — hence the "dirty" moniker — cocktail. A martini garnished with a dill pickle curl? Guaranteed to make anyone smile.

Ingredients:

3 ounces vodka

1 ½ ounces **Bubbies Spicy Dill Pickle** brine

1 ½ ounces vermouth

Bubbies Spicy Dill Pickle curl and olive for garnish

Directions:

1. Fill a cocktail shaker with ice, vodka, pickle brine, and vermouth. Shake well.

2. Strain into a chilled martini glass and garnish with a pickle curl and olive.

Makes 1 cocktail • Total Preparation Time 5 minutes

"A good meal fills the heart as well as the stomach."

Entrees & Sides

Grilled Radicchio

Next time you're firing up the grill for steaks or chicken, toss on some wedges of radicchio for a substantial, healthful, and easy-to-make side dish. If you're not familiar with radicchio, you may have thought that the variegated, softball-size heads in the produce section are a type of cabbage. But radicchio, like endive, is actually a chicory, a family of slightly bitter lettuces sturdy enough to stand up to the intense heat of the grill and come out sweeter for the experience. When creating the dressing for the charred purple-red radicchio leaves, I knew my Beet Horseradish and balsamic vinegar would be the perfect match in color and flavor. Sprinkled with toasted walnuts, Grilled Radicchio just might steal the spotlight at your next cookout.

Ingredients:

2 large radicchio — *halved or quartered*

½ cup toasted walnuts — *chopped*

½ cup olive oil

1 small shallot — *minced*

1 teaspoon Dijon mustard

1 tablespoon **Bubbies Beet Horseradish**

2 tablespoons balsamic vinegar

Salt and freshly ground pepper to taste

Directions:

1. Toast walnuts at 400 degrees for 5-7 min.

2. Brush each piece of radicchio with olive oil. Sprinkle with salt and pepper.

3. Mix shallots, mustard, beet horseradish, balsamic vinegar, and a pinch of salt and pepper in a bowl. Slowly whisk in olive oil until emulsified. Taste and adjust seasoning if necessary.

4. Heat a grill pan or BBQ. When hot, brush with olive oil.

5. Grill the radicchio until slightly charred on each side. Place on serving platter; drizzle with dressing and sprinkle with toasted walnuts.

Serves 4 people • Total Preparation Time 20 minutes

Cannellini Bean Salad

As little powerhouses of nutrition, white beans can't be beat. They are full of vegetable protein, micronutrients, and fiber. All the good stuff that my son-in-law — who just happens to be a doctor — tells me we need more of in our diet. The only downside to beans is that they can be bland. That's why I've added onion, red pepper, and plenty of my Kosher Dill Pickles to this very versatile salad recipe. It's a delicious vegan main dish just as it is, or add feta, cubed chicken, or tuna for a quick and healthful dinner.

Ingredients:

1 garlic clove — *minced*

1 teaspoon Dijon mustard

1 teaspoon **Bubbies Kosher Dill Pickle** brine

¼ cup red wine vinegar

1 teaspoon honey

⅓ cup olive oil

2 cans cannellini beans (rinsed and drained if canned) or roughly 1 cup dried, soaked, cooked for 1-2 hours, and cooled

½ cup **Bubbies Naturally Fermented Kosher Dill Pickles** — *chopped*

½ cup red onion — *chopped*

½ cup roasted red pepper — *chopped*

⅓ cup fresh parsley — *chopped*

2-3 cups fresh arugula or mixed greens

Optional ½ teaspoon Sumac

Salt and freshly ground pepper

Directions:

1. To make the dressing, combine garlic, mustard, pickle brine, vinegar, and honey. Slowly whisk in the olive oil and add a pinch of salt and pepper. Taste and adjust if necessary.

2. In a medium bowl combine all remaining ingredients except the arugula. Add half the dressing and toss. Taste test and add more dressing if desired. Serve over bed of arugula and sprinkle with sumac.

Serves 4 people • Total Preparation Time 20 minutes

Buffalo Chicken Tacos

In Yiddish, a "nosh" is a light meal, often served on a bagel. Substitute a tortilla for the bagel and you have a southwestern-style nosh. When I was a girl, newly arrived on America's shores, I'd never heard of tacos. Likewise, buffalo chicken wings. As I grew older, I loved combining our family's traditional recipes with new flavors I encountered. So when I put tacos and chicken wings together — with slices of my naturally fermented kosher dill pickles — I discovered that I had the perfect nosh for a brunch or a party.
One that made me kvell with pride and my guests shout "Ole!"

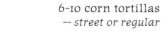

Ingredients:

3-4 cups rotisserie chicken or other cooked chicken — *shredded*

1 cup buffalo sauce of your choice

1 cup Cotija cheese — *crumbled*

1 cup fresh cilantro — *chopped*

3-4 radishes — *sliced thinly*

1 scallion — *sliced thinly*

3 Bubbies Spicy Kosher Dill Pickles — *sliced into small spears*

½ cup sour cream for garnish

1 tablespoon olive oil

6-10 corn tortillas — *street or regular*

Directions:

1. Shred chicken and place in sauté pan with buffalo sauce over medium heat until warm.

2. Prepare all fresh ingredients and set aside in bowls.

3. To soften and brown tortillas, heat olive oil in a medium sauté pan over medium heat and sauté one at a time until lightly browned.

4. Layer all ingredients in tortilla and garnish with pickle spears.

Serves 4 people • Total Preparation Time 20 minutes

Bubbie's Pancetta Burger

Even when you love to cook, there are times when the age-old question of "What's for dinner?" can leave you stumped. Perhaps, like me, you've had the frustrating experience of making loops around the grocery store aisles, zombie-like, and still coming up empty-handed. For times like this, I've made the ultimate beef burger my go-to dinner solution. It's quick to prepare, flavorful, and guaranteed to make the family happy. And when served with Bubbie's Special Sauce, it rivals the $22 burger on the fanciest restaurant menu.

Ingredients:

½ cup mayonnaise (preferably homemade aioli)

2 tablespoons **Bubbies Kosher Dill Relish**

1 small garlic clove — *minced*

2 teaspoons ketchup

1 tablespoon **Bubbies Prepared Horseradish**

2 onions
— *halved and sliced ¼ inch thick*

1 teaspoon balsamic vinegar

4 thin slices pancetta

1 ¼ lbs of ground beef chuck 80/20

2 garlic cloves — *crushed*

4-6 leaves butter lettuce

1 tomato — *thinly sliced*

4 slices aged white cheddar

4 soft hamburger buns — *toasted*

Olive oil

Salt and freshly ground pepper

Directions:

1. To make Bubbies Special Sauce: combine mayo, relish, minced garlic, ketchup, and horseradish in a small bowl. Refrigerate until ready to serve.

2. In a heavy skillet over medium heat, heat 2 tablespoons olive oil. Add onions and cook for about 5 minutes. Add a sprinkle of salt and pepper.

3. Turn down heat and continue to cook until nicely caramelized, about 15 more minutes. About halfway through, add 1 teaspoon balsamic vinegar. Set aside to cool.

4. Cook pancetta to desired crispness; reserve drippings and set aside.

5. In a bowl mix beef with crushed garlic, salt, and pepper. Mix just a few times to incorporate. Don't over mix.

6. Heat skillet to medium high. Add a tablespoon of the pancetta drippings. When hot, add burgers and cook 5-7 minutes on each side for medium burgers. Watch heat; lower a bit if pan gets too hot. Add cheese after 3 minutes of cooking on second side.

7. Toast buns. Remove burgers to a platter. Let your guests build their burgers with all the fixings.

Serves 4 people • Total Preparation Time 45 min

Pulled Pork Sliders

Pulled pork has become very popular for many reasons: it's a crowd-pleasing dish that doesn't require any last-minute preparation, and the combination of seasonings hits our tangy, smoky, and sweet spot. But, unlike many recipes, you won't find my pulled pork swimming in a super-syrupy sauce. I give it a nice massage with a dry rub, then marinate it in olive oil and orange juice — or any citrus you like — for a brighter flavor. Serve it with zingy homemade barbeque sauce, crunchy shredded cabbage, and plenty of my sweet Bread & Butter Chips for an easy entrée guaranteed to make the crowd go wild.

Ingredients:

Pulled Pork:

3-pound boneless pork roast — *marinated overnight*

1 small napa cabbage — *thinly sliced*

2 cups **Bubbies Bread & Butter Pickles**

12-15 small slider buns — *toasted*

2 cups water or stock

Rub for Pork:

1 tablespoon cumin

1 tablespoon smoked paprika

1 tablespoon dried oregano

2 tablespoons salt

1 teaspoon pepper

3 garlic cloves — *crushed*

2 tablespoons olive oil

½ cup citrus juice — *orange, lemon, and lime*

BBQ Sauce:

¾ cup ketchup

½ cup water

¼ cup apple cider vinegar

½ teaspoon salt and pepper

1 teaspoon smoked paprika

1 teaspoon dried mustard powder

¼ teaspoon cumin

1 ½ tablespoons Worcestershire sauce

1 teaspoon chili powder

1 tablespoon maple syrup

½ cup onions — *minced*

2 garlic cloves — *minced*

Directions:

1. Combine all ingredients for the rub and rub onto pork. Place in plastic ziplock bag and refrigerate overnight or 4-6 hours. Set pork on the counter for 1-2 hours before cooking.

2. Heat oven to 300 degrees. Over high heat, heat olive oil in an enamel or heavy stock pot with lid, and sear all sides of pork well. Add the stock to pork. Cover and place in oven for 3-4 hours until pork easily pulls apart. If you have an Instant Pot you can cook the pork in 1½ hours.

3. While the pork is cooking, prepare the BBQ sauce: Combine all sauce ingredients in a small pan and simmer for 15 minutes. Puree with an immersion blender.

4. To serve, combine pork and half the sauce. Toast buns. Put small amount of cabbage on bottom of each bun and spoon pulled pork over cabbage. Add bread and butter pickles. Top with bun and serve, with extra sauce on the side.

Serves 7-10 people • Total Preparation Time 4 hrs

German-Inspired Pizza

A few years ago, I was enjoying the brats and beer at an Oktoberfest party when, between the polkas, I started thinking about the traditional German foods on my plate. Could they be transformed into an easy-to-eat main course that would be at home in an American kitchen? I knew the combination of flavors would be delicious, but what would hold it all together? That's when inspiration struck. Turn a pretzel into pizza dough base, then pile on the savory bratwurst. Toss on some slices of small white potatoes, add sweet apples, and top it off with my crunchy kraut. It's a party on your plate.

Ingredients:

2 teaspoons rapid-rising yeast

1½ teaspoons salt

4 cups flour

1½ cups warm water — *divided*

1 tablespoon olive oil

You can also use your favorite store-bought pizza dough

6-7 little white or red potatoes

2 bratwurst (remove casings)

3-4 large shallots, about 2 cups — *sliced*

4 tablespoons butter

2 tablespoons white cooking wine

½ - ¾ cup heavy cream

1 apple (Gravenstein, Gala, Empire or Granny Smith) — *thinly sliced*

2 cups shredded Fontina cheese

1 cup **Bubbies Naturally Fermented Sauerkraut** — *drained*

Directions:

1. To make dough: place ¼ cup warm water in a small bowl and sprinkle with yeast. Let sit for 5 minutes until yeast is hydrated and creamy.

2. In the bowl of an electric mixer fitted with a dough hook, place flour, salt, yeast mixture, olive oil and remaining 1¼ cups warm water. Mix on low speed for 2-3 minutes to combine. If dough appears too wet and sticky add flour, 1 tablespoon at a time, mixing until dough comes together to form a ball. Dough should still be moist but not too sticky.

3. Remove dough hook. Cover dough with plastic wrap and let rise for 1-2 hours until doubled in size. While dough is rising, prepare the pizza toppings.

4. Preheat oven to 475 degrees, with pizza stone if available.

5. To make pizza: steam potatoes for 7-10 minutes, then remove from heat to cool. Don't cook them completely; they should have a slight hardness in center.

6. Remove bratwurst from casing and cook over medium heat until done. Set aside in bowl.

7. Sauté shallots in butter with a pinch of salt and pepper for 3-5 minutes on medium heat until caramelized. Add wine and deglaze pan.

Serves 2-4 • Total Preparation Time 2½ hours

8. Add cream and simmer shallots for 3-5 minutes until thickened. Add more cream for desired thickness; remove from heat and set aside.

9. Thinly slice potatoes and apples.

10. Divide dough into 2 equal balls. Roll out each dough ball and transfer to a baking sheet or pizza pan sprinkled with cornmeal or flour so the dough doesn't stick. Lightly brush dough with olive oil. Spread creamy shallots evenly onto dough, leaving about ½-1 inch from border.

11. Add cheese, apples, potatoes, and sausage. Transfer pizza to oven, either onto the hot stone or in pizza pan.

12. Bake 10-15 minutes until crust is brown and cheese is melted.

13. Top with sauerkraut and enjoy!

Tempura-Style Fried Fish

One of the fascinating things about food is that similar recipes are found in cultures around the globe. People the world over agree that crispy, beer-battered fish is delicious whether cooked tempura-style in Japan, served with chips in Britain's most iconic dish, or fried up on Fridays in Eastern European kitchens to be eaten cold on Shabbat. Served with tangy tartar sauce that gets a little heat from my horseradish, this mouthwatering dish might even be out of this world — it's that good.

Ingredients:

1 to 1½ pounds white-fleshed fish — *cut into 2-inch x 3-inch pieces*

2 cups all-purpose flour

2 tablespoons cornstarch

1 tablespoon baking powder

12 ounces beer (your choice)

2 cups panko breadcrumbs

½ cup mayonnaise

½ cup Greek yogurt

¼ cup **Bubbies Prepared Horseradish**

1 tablespoon Worcestershire sauce

⅛ cup lemon juice

½ cup **Bubbies Kosher Dill Relish**

1 tablespoon **Bubbies Kosher Dill Pickle** brine

Salt and white pepper to taste

Oil for frying

Lemon — *cut into wedges*

Directions:

1. To make sauce for dipping: combine mayonnaise, yogurt, horseradish, Worcestershire, lemon juice, relish, brine, salt, and pepper. Refrigerate.

2. Prepare batter by combining flour, cornstarch, baking powder, and beer. Put panko into a shallow dish for dipping.

3. Prepare the fish by removing any bones and salting. Slice into 2-inch x 3-inch pieces.

4. Heat oil in deep fryer or deep stock pot.

5. Dip each piece of fish into batter, then roll in panko. Carefully place into hot oil for frying.

6. Cook until golden brown and set on paper towels to absorb excess oil.

7. Serve with French fries, lemon wedges, and tartar sauce.

Serves 4 people • Total Preparation Time 30 minutes

Horseradish Chicken Pot Pies

Does anything look more tempting than a glossy and beautifully browned pie crust? It practically cries out to the diner to grab a knife and slice into the flaky layers to reveal the deliciousness inside. This flavorful recipe for classic comfort food won't disappoint. Filled with colorful vegetables and a sauce that blends white wine with a generous helping of my horseradish, this dish is sophisticated enough to serve to guests. And because it starts with frozen puff pastry and cooked chicken (rotisserie chicken from the store works just great), once the vegetables are chopped, the recipe comes together surprisingly quick. If you're feeling ambitious, serve it with a salad. Otherwise, one dish and you're done!

Ingredients:

1 package frozen puff pastry — *thawed*

8 ounces cooked chicken cut into 1-inch pieces (thighs or breasts)

½ cup **Bubbies Prepared Horseradish**

2 tablespoons fresh thyme

2 carrots cut into 1-inch pieces

2 cups fresh green beans cut into 2-inch pieces
(if green beans aren't in season use 1 cup frozen peas)

1 leek (white and pale green parts only), washed and drained and cut into ½ inch half moons

1 russet potato, peeled and cut into small ½ inch cubes

2 cups mushrooms sliced into 1-inch pieces

½ fennel bulb — *sliced thinly*

3 tablespoons butter — *softened*

3 tablespoons flour

1½-2 cups chicken stock

½ cup white wine

Olive oil

Salt and pepper

Egg wash for pastry

4-6 individual ovenproof ramekins about 8-10 ounces in size

Directions:

1. Preheat oven to 400 degrees. Place thawed pastry dough on a piece of parchment paper or a lightly floured surface. With a rolling pin roll the dough slightly thinner, a few rolls in each direction. Place a ramekin upside down on the dough and cut a circle slightly larger than the ramekin; continue for each ramekin. Place on parchment-lined baking sheet and refrigerate until ready to use.

2. Prepare egg wash: whisk one egg with a splash of cold water or milk until mixed.

3. For the filling: Heat olive oil in a large 4-inch deep skillet over medium heat; cook the leeks and carrots with a pinch of

salt until slightly softened, about 3 minutes. Add green beans, mushrooms, fennel, thyme, and potato (add a bit more olive oil if necessary), and cook for 3-5 minutes. Place vegetables in a large bowl and set aside.

4. Make a slurry with 3 tablespoons softened butter mixed with 3 tablespoons flour. Cream together and set aside. In the same skillet over medium heat add wine and deglaze the pan, scraping any bits from bottom of the pan. Add 1½ cups stock and whisk in butter/flour mixture. Continue cooking and stirring occasionally until thickened, about 5 minutes. Add horseradish and stir well.

5. Add vegetables and chicken back into skillet and cook another 5 minutes. Taste and adjust seasoning with salt and freshly ground pepper. If the sauce is too thick, add up to ½ cup more stock to desired consistency.

6. Divide mixture evenly among ramekins (if using frozen peas stir about ¼ cup into each). Using a pastry brush or your finger, brush egg wash around the top of the ramekin; this will help to seal crust to the ramekin.

7. Top each dish with a puff pastry round and press down to seal. Place ramekins on a baking sheet and brush tops with egg wash. Use a knife to make a small slit in top of each pastry. Bake until crust is golden, about 20-25 minutes. Let cool 5-10 minutes before serving.

Serves 4 • Total Preparation Time 50 minutes

Beef Stroganoff

When I was growing up, stroganoff was a trendy dish. Like today's obsession with quinoa and kale, you couldn't open a newspaper or magazine without seeing a recipe for it. My mother – an excellent cook in her own right – created her own version with her homemade horseradish. I liked it so much that stroganoff was the dish I always asked her to make for my birthday dinner. Though stroganoff has fallen out of fashion, the combination of sautéed thinly sliced beef, meaty mushrooms, red wine, tangy sour cream, and my Spicy Horseradish makes an umami-packed, surprisingly quick-to-prepare entrée that is worth rediscovering. I hope it will be a favorite in your home too.

Ingredients:

1 Sirloin or Strip Steak, about 1 to 1½ pounds
— *sliced ¼ inch thick by 1 inch long*

2 onions — *halved and thinly sliced*

1 tablespoon thyme leaves

2 tablespoons butter

1 pound mushrooms — *thinly sliced*

3 garlic cloves — *chopped*

1 pound egg noodles — *cooked al dente according to package directions*

½ cup red wine

2 tablespoons flour + 2 tablespoons butter combined into a paste

1 ½ cups beef broth

½ cup **Bubbies Spicy Horseradish**

1 cup sour cream

1 tablespoon lemon juice

¼ cup fresh dill for garnish

Salt and pepper

Olive oil

Directions:

1. In a large skillet, heat 2 tablespoons of olive oil over medium heat. Add onions and sauté until brown and caramelized about 15-20 minutes, stirring occasionally. Add thyme leaves and sauté 2 more minutes. Transfer to a bowl and set aside.

2. Add 2 tablespoons butter or olive oil to skillet. Add mushrooms and sauté 5-7 minutes over medium-high heat until they release their juices and soften. Add garlic and sauté 2 more minutes. Transfer to a bowl and set aside.

3. In a large pot, bring water to a boil and cook egg noodles *al dente*. Strain.

4. Sprinkle meat with salt and pepper. Brown in a pan with olive oil over medium-high heat in two batches. Transfer to a bowl when done. Set aside.

5. Deglaze pan with ½ cup red wine; cook and reduce by half, scraping bits from bottom of pan, about 3 minutes. Whisk in flour/butter paste and beef broth until well incorporated. Cook about 5 minutes more until thickened. Add beef back to pan and cook a few more minutes until heated through.

6. Add mushrooms, caramelized onions, and lemon juice to pan and stir together. Cook for 2 more minutes. Add horseradish and sour cream. Stir just until combined and warmed. Taste and adjust seasoning if necessary.

7. Garnish with fresh dill and serve immediately over noodles.

Serves 4-6 people • Total Preparation Time 1 hour

Herb-Crusted Rack of Lamb

When planning your next dinner party menu, what could be better than a show-stopping entrée that doesn't need a lot of attention at the last minute? Serving a rack of lamb makes portioning easy – something that can be problematic with other roasted meats such as chicken and pork. The recipe starts by searing the rack and then patting on the coating to keep it extra juicy. When served, the crunchy texture of the hazelnut, horseradish and breadcrumb crust contrasts perfectly with the tender lamb. Elegant and easy.

Ingredients:

2 racks of lamb – *bones trimmed and frenched*

⅓ cup **Bubbies Prepared Horseradish**
(press out all excess brine)

½ cup hazelnuts – *toasted, skinned and finely chopped*

¼ cup breadcrumbs or panko

3 garlic cloves – *minced*

2 tablespoons fresh mint
– *finely chopped*

1 tablespoon fresh oregano
– *finely chopped*

1 tablespoon fresh rosemary
– *finely chopped*

3 tablespoons olive oil

1 teaspoon sea salt

½ teaspoon freshly
ground pepper

Directions:

1. Preheat oven to 400 degrees.

2. Trim each rack of excess fat and season with salt and pepper. Let rest on a baking sheet at room temperature for 30-45 minutes.

3. Toast hazelnuts in oven for about 8-10 minutes. Let cool, then rub together with a kitchen cloth; this will remove most of the skins. Don't worry about removing all. Finely chop or pulse in a food processor.

4. To make crust, combine horseradish, hazelnuts, crumbs, garlic, herbs, salt and pepper.

5. Heat 2 tablespoons oil in a large ovenproof skillet on medium-high heat. When the oil is hot add one lamb rack, meat side down, and sear well on each side and end. Set aside and sear the second rack.

6. Brush each rack with olive oil and coat each rack with the crust, patting the mixture a bit so it sticks. Arrange each rack crust side up on a baking sheet or in the same skillet and roast for 20-25 minutes. Insert a thermometer and check for desired doneness (125 degrees for rare). Let racks rest for about 5 minutes before carving.

7. Cut each lamb rack between the bones and serve.

Serves 4-6 people • Total Preparation Time 1 hour 15 minutes

Winter Stew

Isn't it amazing that stew, one of the world's oldest comfort foods, can be made from just two ingredients simmered in a liquid? While that is the bare-bones recipe, making a really soul-satisfying stew requires a few more ingredients, maybe even one that is a little unexpected. That's where my Naturally Fermented Sauerkraut comes in. Its tang and texture are the perfect complement to the sweetness of the vegetables. Add a little more sauerkraut on top for garnish and you've got a stew that will chase the chill from any winter night.

Ingredients:

1 pound stew meat
— *cut into ½ inch pieces*

1-2 tablespoons flour

2 tablespoons olive oil

1 onion — *chopped*

2 carrots — *sliced ½ inch*

2 garlic cloves — *chopped*

2 celery stalks — *sliced ¼ inch*

½ cup red wine

2 tablespoons tomato paste

1 quart beef stock

2 cups **Bubbies Naturally Fermented Sauerkraut** + ½ cup brine

1 small sweet potato — *cut into ½-inch chunks*

2 small red potatoes — *cut into ½-inch chunks*

½ pound mushrooms — *quartered*

2 cups pearl onions — *skins removed* (Place onions in boiling water for 3-5 minutes, then peel off skins)

2 bay leaves

4 sprigs of thyme — *stemmed*

Salt and pepper

Directions:

1. To prepare meat: salt, pepper, and dust with flour to coat all sides. Put olive oil in a dutch oven over medium heat. Add meat in two batches, and brown on all sides. Set aside in a bowl.

2. Add more olive oil to the same pot, and sauté onion, carrots, garlic, and celery with a pinch of salt and pepper for 3-5 minutes, stirring often.

3. Add red wine and deglaze, scraping bits from bottom of the pan, until wine is reduced by half.

4. Add tomato paste and stir until dissolved, then add beef stock, ½ cup sauerkraut brine, potatoes, mushrooms, pearl onions, bay leaves, thyme and the meat — cover and cook over a low simmer for 20-25 minutes. If stew is too thick, add more stock; if it's too thin, mix 1-2 tablespoons flour with ¼ cup warm stock until dissolved, add to stew and mix well.

5. Continue to cook on low for 15 more minutes until vegetables are done and flavors are blended. Taste and adjust seasoning if necessary.

6. Garnish each bowl with a heaping tablespoon of Bubbies Naturally Fermented Sauerkraut.

Serves 4 people • Total Preparation Time 1 hour

"You did leave room for dessert didn't you dear?"

Desserts

Sauer Apple Strudel

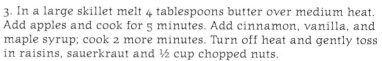

Apples and cabbage, both at their peak in the fall, have a natural affinity for each other. The combination is found in many traditional German side dishes. I grew up eating braised cabbage and apples, typically made with a touch of vinegar. I loved the sweet-and-sour combination so it seemed a natural progression to incorporate crisp sauerkraut into the filling of my favorite apple strudel recipe for added tang and texture. The result? Stru-delicious!

Ingredients:

4 large apples (Granny Smith or other tart apple) — *peeled and sliced into ¼ inch wedges*

1 tablespoon fresh lemon juice

4 tablespoons (½ stick) unsalted butter

1 teaspoon cinnamon

1 teaspoon vanilla

½ cup maple syrup or sugar

½ cup golden raisins

½ cup raisins (or substitute dried cranberries or cherries)

1 cup **Bubbies Naturally Fermented Sauerkraut**

½ cup walnuts — *toasted and chopped*

1 package phyllo dough — *thawed according to directions on box*

½ cup (1 stick) unsalted butter — *melted*

½ cup toasted walnuts — *finely chopped*

1 tablespoon turbinado sugar

Directions:

1. Preheat oven to 400 degrees.

2. Prepare apples and toss in a bowl with fresh lemon juice.

3. In a large skillet melt 4 tablespoons butter over medium heat. Add apples and cook for 5 minutes. Add cinnamon, vanilla, and maple syrup; cook 2 more minutes. Turn off heat and gently toss in raisins, sauerkraut and ½ cup chopped nuts.

4. Pour mixture onto a baking sheet and spread out to cool while preparing dough.

5. Melt ½ cup butter and pour into a shallow dish. Line a baking sheet with parchment. Open phyllo dough and gently unroll. Count out 8 sheets. (Roll the remaining sheets, wrap tightly with plastic wrap, and place in refrigerator for another use.)

6. Place one phyllo sheet on parchment paper, and use pastry brush to brush with butter. Place another sheet on top of buttered one, and continue process 6 more times until all 8 sheets are buttered and layered.

7. Sprinkle ½ cup finely chopped walnuts along long side of dough closest to you, only about 4 inches wide and leaving the ends. Next, take cooled apple mixture and spread over walnuts, again leaving the ends.

8. Now starting on the strudel's filled side, pull it up and begin rolling the dough once. Stop and tuck in the ends, then continue rolling dough to finish with open end on bottom. You will have a nice log.

9. Center strudel on parchment, and generously brush top, sides, and ends with melted butter. Sprinkle generously with turbinado sugar. Bake 30-40 minutes until nicely browned on top.

10. Let cool 15-20 minutes.

Serves 6-8 people • Total Preparation Time 1 hour, 15 minutes

Bubbie's Special Brownies

You're probably thinking, what in the world is sauerkraut doing in a brownie recipe? If you know me, you know there's no "too much of a good thing" when it comes to my Naturally Fermented Sauerkraut. I started experimenting, even adding it to classic American dessert recipes. Sauerkraut in chocolate chip cookies? Not a success. But, amazingly, when I added sauerkraut to brownies, they came out moist, rich, and more chocolatey than before. Give it a try. You may find that thinking outside the jar yields some really delicious results.

Ingredients:

¾ cup (1 ½ sticks) salted butter*

3 eggs

1 cup sugar

½ cup plus 2 tablespoons flour*

½ cup plus 2 tablespoons unsweetened cocoa powder

½ teaspoon baking powder

2 cups **Bubbies Naturally Fermented Sauerkraut** *— drained and finely chopped*

½ cup chopped walnuts or pecans (optional)

¾ cup chocolate chips

*Use gluten-free all-purpose flour and vegan butter for a hypoaller-genic version.

Directions:

1. Preheat oven to 350 degrees. Spray a 9-inch x 9-inch baking pan with cooking spray, or coat with butter or cooking oil.

2. In a medium saucepan, melt butter over medium heat. Stir in sugar until blended, about 2 minutes. Remove from heat and beat in eggs one at a time, mixing well after each addition.

3. In a medium bowl, mix the flour, cocoa powder, and baking powder. Add flour mixture to butter mixture, stirring until combined.

4. Stir in sauerkraut, nuts, and chocolate chips.

5. Spread mixture into prepared pan. Bake 30-40 minutes until center is set.

6. Cool completely before cutting.

Serves 6 people • Total Preparation Time 50 minutes

Candied Sauerkraut Truffles

My family often says, "Bubbie, there's nothing you like more than a challenge." I suppose that's true because, after my success with Sauerkraut Brownies, I immediately started wondering what next uncharted culinary territory I could venture into. Appetizers, soups, main dishes, cocktails, and now even desserts — my Naturally Fermented Sauerkraut has been there and done that, often with delicious results. But candy? That's a challenge I could sink my teeth into. I discovered that candying my kraut and combining it with ganache makes truffles with a certain *je ne sais quoi*. Want to have some fun? Serve them at your next party and have your guests guess the secret ingredient.

Ingredients:

Candied Sauerkraut:

½ cup **Bubbies Naturally Fermented Sauerkraut**

1 ¼ cup sugar

Chocolate Ganache:

8 ounces dark chocolate — *chopped or chips*

½ cup heavy cream

¼ cup unsweetened cocoa powder — *optional*

Directions:

1. Preheat oven to 400 degrees.

2. Measure ½ cup of sauerkraut and drain well, then squeeze sauerkraut with your hands to remove most of the remaining brine.

3. Put sauerkraut into a bowl with sugar and toss until sauerkraut is completely covered.

4. Place sugared sauerkraut on a parchment-lined baking sheet and place in oven until sauerkraut is caramelized and golden, about 4-7 minutes. Keep a close eye on it as it can darken quickly.

5. Let it cool while making ganache: Bring cream to a simmer in a small saucepan. Remove from heat and stir in chocolate until smooth. Pour chocolate mixture into an 8-inch glass baking dish and let sit for 8-10 minutes.

6. Chop cooled candied sauerkraut and stir into chocolate. Cover with plastic wrap and place in refrigerator until chilled, about 20-30 minutes.

7. Using a 1-inch ice cream scoop, melon baller, or tablespoon, scoop chocolate into balls. Optional: Roll in cocoa powder, and shake off excess. Makes 20-25 truffles.

Serves 6 people • Total Preparation Time 1 hour

"Meyn Balibste"
(My Beloved)

Kathy's Favorites

Homemade Mustard

If the entrée is the star of the meal, condiments are the backup singers – enhancing the dish's flavor without stealing the spotlight. That just might change when you serve this creamy, piquant mustard. As much a sauce as an accompaniment, it has a million uses. I love it as a dip for crudités, as a sauce to spoon over chicken, pork, ham, fish, or steamed broccoli, or as a condiment for hot dogs, sausages, and pretzels.

Ingredients:

1 cup dry Coleman Mustard

1 cup apple cider vinegar

1 cup sugar

2 egg yolks

Directions:

1. Mix dry mustard and apple cider vinegar in a heatproof bowl and let sit for 2 hours.

2. Whisk in sugar and egg yolks. Place the bowl over a pot of simmering water, but do not let the bowl touch the water. Cook slowly 1 hour, stirring occasionally.

3. Let cool and pour into jars.

Makes 8 ounces • Total Preparation Time 4 hours

Kathy's Tuna Salad

Coleslaw meets tuna salad for a delicious and healthful sandwich filling.
Or serve the salad on a bed of greens for a light dinner. The red cabbage adds
extra crunch, color, and nutrients while my Dill Pickle Relish brings zing.
Want to lighten it up even more? Substitute Greek yogurt for the mayo.

Ingredients:

5-ounce can tuna

2-3 tablespoons mayonnaise

2 tablespoons **Bubbies Kosher Dill Relish**

¼ cup red cabbage
— *thinly chopped*

¼ cup onion or scallions
(or both with some of the
greens) — *chopped*

Salt and pepper to taste

Directions:

1. Drain tuna.
2. Place all ingredients in a bowl and toss together, if necessary adding a bit more of whatever suits your taste.

Serves 4 people • Total Preparation Time 10 minutes

Split Pea Soup

For a satisfying supper, you can't beat a recipe that has just one line of directions: put ingredients in a pot and ignore them for a couple of hours while the split peas do their magic and turn into a creamy, rich soup. I like Split Pea Soup so much that I've been known to eat it for breakfast. In the unlikely case that you run out of appetite before you run out of soup, it freezes beautifully.

Ingredients:

1 onion — *chopped*

1 cup celery with leaves — *chopped*

1 cup carrots — *chopped*

1 clove garlic — *chopped*

16-ounce package split peas — *rinsed*

1 ham bone or ham shank

2 ½ quarts chicken stock or water, or a combo of both

1 bay leaf

1 tablespoon fresh thyme

Dash of cayenne — *optional*

Salt and pepper

Olive oil

Directions:

1. Place a large soup pot over medium heat and add olive oil, onion, celery, carrots, garlic, and salt and pepper; sauté for 3-5 minutes. 2. Add split peas, ham bone, stock, bay leaf, and thyme. Bring to a simmer for 1-2 hours, stirring periodically. 3. Remove bone from ham and discard. The soup can then be left as is with the ham added, or you can purée the soup and then add the ham. 4. Taste and adjust seasoning if necessary.

Serves 4 people • Total Preparation Time 1-2 hours

Lentil Soup

One of the earliest crops cultivated in the Old World, lentils made a hearty and filling meal long before Aristotle cooked up a batch. A few thousand years later, I used lentils as the base for a flavorful, stick-to-the-ribs soup loaded with aromatic vegetables and salty-sweet ham. In a hurry? Omit the bacon and just toss all the other ingredients in the pot. Those lovely legumes will be tender in about an hour.

Ingredients:

1 16-ounce package lentils

4 ounces bacon — *chopped, optional*

2 cups carrots — *diced*

2 onions — *diced*

1 cup celery — *diced*

1 large potato — *peeled and cut into small chunks*

2 quarts vegetable broth, chicken stock, or water

1 ham bone or ham shank

2 teaspoons fresh thyme

2 bay leaves

Salt and pepper

Olive oil

Directions:

1. If using bacon, begin by cooking it until crisp. Remove from pan and place on paper towel.

2. Sauté carrots, onion, and celery with a pinch of salt and pepper for 3-5 minutes in olive oil or remaining bacon drippings.

3. Rinse lentils and add to pot with potato, stock, ham bone, thyme, and bay leaves.

4. Simmer about 1 hour, stirring periodically. Remove meat from ham bone; discard bone and return ham to pot. Stir in bacon, saving a little for garnish. Taste and adjust seasoning if necessary.

Serves 4 people • Total Preparation Time 1 hour 15 minutes

Chocolate Walnut Tart

Why serve ordinary pumpkin pie on Thanksgiving when your guests will swoon over a chocolatey, nutty, absolutely yummy tart instead? It starts with an easy shortbread crust that comes together quickly in the food processor, and it's topped with a filling that requires no stovetop cooking. If the tart isn't rich enough, you can always gild the lily and serve it with homemade vanilla sauce or whipped cream.

butter

Pastry:

Ingredients:

1 9-inch tart pan

¾ cup flour

¼ cup powdered (confectioners) sugar

3 tablespoons chilled cut into small pieces

1 egg whisked in a small bowl

Directions:

1. Put all ingredients except the egg into food processor and run 30 seconds, then add one-third to one-half of the egg and continue to run until a ball is formed. Save remaining egg for filling.

2. Place dough in plastic wrap and form into a disk. Refrigerate 30 min.

3. Roll out dough, dusting with powdered sugar, then press into bottom of tart pan and up sides 1 inch. Chill again before adding filling.

Filling:

Ingredients:

2 eggs plus leftover egg from pastry dough

⅔ cup brown sugar — *packed*

⅔ cup Karo corn syrup

2 tablespoons melted butter

1 teaspoon vanilla

6 ounces semisweet chocolate chips — *melted*

1 cup toasted walnuts — *chopped*

Directions:

1. Mix eggs, sugar, corn syrup, butter and vanilla together in a bowl. Add chopped nuts and melted chocolate. Pour into chilled tart dough.

2. Bake at 350 degrees for 30-40 minutes until set in middle. Cool before serving.

Vanilla Sauce, optional:

1 cup milk

4 egg yolks

¼ cup sugar

vanilla or Kahlua

Directions:

1. Heat milk in a medium saucepan over medium heat, but don't let it boil. In a bowl, whisk together egg yolks and sugar. Slowly whisk hot milk into egg mixture, a little at a time, until all milk is added. Return mixture to saucepan and cook slowly, stirring constantly, until thickened, about 5 minutes. Strain into bowl and add vanilla, Kahlua or other flavoring. Enjoy!

Serves 6 • Total Preparation Time About 1 hour 15 minutes

A sneak peek...

behind the scenes of Bubbies Kitchen and Cookbook shoot.

To find more recipes and videos, visit us at bubbies.com!

Cornmeal Crusted
Calamari
Page 19

Pickled
Whiskey Sour
Page 41

Buffalo
Chicken Tacos
Page 51

Sauer
Apple Strudel
Page 71

Index of Ingredients